FRENCHMAN'S BAY

FRENCHMAN'S

Photography by *Edgar B. Van Winkle*, Text by *Elizabeth Simonoff*

A Publication of The Coleraine Press, Inc.,
published by The Pequot Press, Inc., Chester, Connecticut

Copyright © 1973 *Edgar B. Van Winkle* and *Elizabeth Simonoff*.
Library of Congress Card Number 73-80885. ISBN 87106-117-1.
Manufactured in the United States of America.
All rights reserved. First Edition.

BAY

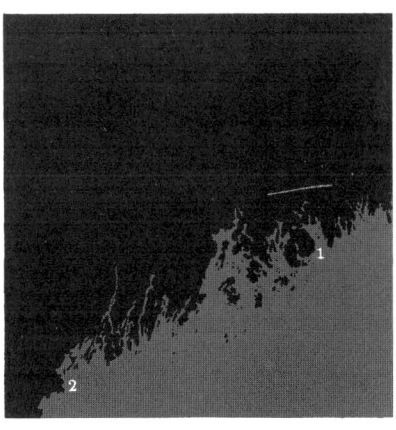

Frenchman's Bay[1] lies 100 nautical miles from the Portland,[2] Maine, lightship on a "down-east" bearing of 60° true or approximately North East by East ¼ East.

WATER

Whether you come by road or sea, Frenchman's Bay, at first sight, takes you by surprise. Stretching north seven miles from its Atlantic headlands, its color shifting with the weather, its mountain rim of wind-scoured granite plunging steeply into the water, the bay seems shaped to a different scale, with a broader reach and bolder contrasts than the surrounding coast. The cautionary names given its promontories and islands by early settlers—Schooner Head, Black Ledge, Ironbound, Bald Rock, the Porcupine Islands—describe the shore as it appears to the inbound sailor, easing his boat up the channel between markers for reefs and ledges. But the motorist's view from Route 1 at the head of the bay encompasses more than is visible from the water. There, at a high point in the road, a vast panorama stretches seaward: an arm of the ocean from which blue-shadowed mountains rise like dark bubbles in the early evening, taking their color from the northern sky, or on foggy mornings, their crests floating spectrally above the mist-blanketed water. Frenchman's Bay is different—harsher, wilder, and more beautiful—than the other bays along the Maine coast. Its western headland, Mount Desert Island, ascends summit behind summit to 1530-foot Cadillac Mountain, the highest point on the United States eastern seaboard. Schoodic Point, opposite Mount Desert across the bay, is a surf-battered rock peninsula known to naturalists for its Arctic plant life, which includes species seldom found south of Labrador. Immense boulders lie strewn like pebbles along the tide line of these outer headlands, wrenched from the cliffs by winter storms. Waves pound the rock, their tempo changing with the wind; tides rise and ebb; silver herring appear at the mouth of the bay one morning and are mys-

teriously gone the next; gulls endlessly scream and dive. ⁓This landscape with its granite skeleton exposed in mountain domes and headlands, looks as if it has survived unchanged from the time the earth was formed. But if you measure time by geologic rather than human history, the bay's shoreline and the contours of its mountains are actually rather new. ⁓Up to a million and a half years ago, the Mount Desert range was a single, high ridge, reaching inland from a coast that lay east of the present shore, its north and south slopes grooved by the beds of tumbling highland brooks. Its summits and valleys were carved out by the glacier that pushed eastward from the Arctic across the continent, forcing its way over the plains and up the mountainsides of what is now New England, crushing forests, rolling off topsoil, and dragging with it great boulders that reamed the surface of the land. ⁓With the grindstones embedded in its underside, the glacier smoothed and rounded the northwest faces of the mountains around Frenchman's Bay. When the ice sheet reached its greatest thickness, the entire ridge lay buried under a mile-deep crust and remained that way for thousands of years, during which time the glacier's enormous weight depressed the eastern edge of the continent, tilting it toward the ocean. ⁓Finally, slow climatic changes melted the glacier. The accumulating water freed by what must have been the greatest thaw the continent has ever seen, raised the level of the sea and flooded former coastal lowlands, advancing up river valleys, submerging the old shoreline and creating a new one. ⁓ Today the sloops and launches of summer folk thread their way across the bay between islands that were hills along the older coast. And, summer and winter, the fishermen of Bar Harbor, Win-

SHORE

ter Harbor, Sorrento, and other towns and hamlets around the bay, build their weirs in the shallows and pull their lobster traps in the deeper water that covers the pre-glacial coastal plain. ~ Some years ago a young man from Lamoine, a fishing and farming community at the head of Frenchman's Bay, was signed by a major league baseball team. Raised in the Lamoine Little League, the pride of his coaches, he was given a grand send-off by the entire town when he left for training. ~ A few weeks after his departure, the youth was back in Lamoine. Stricken with homesickness for the bay and the country around it that has afflicted others before and since, he had decided to relinquish his chance for a baseball career, and had packed and headed home. ~ The bay is a place people have been coming back to since the Abnaki Indians of inland Maine discovered the abundant food it offered in summer. They came to its shores each year to fish and dig clams; today deep shell heaps still mark their long abandoned camp grounds in a number of spots on the bay's periphery. ~ Historians differ over which European explorers of the New World were the first to sight the rocky domes of Mount Desert, visible from 60 miles at sea. Some believe that Norsemen sailing from Newfoundland came to the area around the year 1000; others say the Portuguese, Estaban Gomes, was the first in 1525. ~ But the earliest documented account of a landfall on the shore of Frenchman's Bay itself was that of Samuel de Champlain, who explored the Maine coast in the autumn of 1604. Champlain crossed the bay on September 6 of that year, pausing for boat repairs at the mouth of the stream now called Otter Creek on Mount Desert, after grounding on a nearby reef. Impressed by the island's rock domes, he called it l'Isle des

Monts-deserts, (the island of the bare mountains), the name it bears in anglicized form today. ◦‿Champlain's visit began a century and a half of French influence around the bay, bringing to its shores the succession of swashbuckling warrior-sailors for whom it was named, and making it today the only place in the United States other than Louisiana where land titles are traced back to the French crown. He had been sent to explore the coast by the Sieur de Monts, a nobleman who had a crown grant to l'Acadie (the French version of an Indian word meaning "the place") which embraced the entire French claim in North America. He paused at Mount Desert only long enough to repair his ship and take aboard Indian guides, but he described the island and the bay so accurately in his account of the voyage that later explorers recognized it without difficulty. ◦‿ Nine years later another French expedition came to the bay seeking shelter during a stretch of bad weather. This little band, whose leaders included a Jesuit priest, Pierre Biard, had been financed by an influential Frenchwoman, the Marquise de Guercheville. The Marquise had acquired de Monts' patent and planned to colonize and christianize what was by then optimistically called New France. ◦‿Biard's party sailed up the bay and landed at the site of present day Cromwell's Cove on the east side of Mount Desert Island, planting a cross and naming the spot Saint-Sauveur. Soon after their landing, the French were approached by Indians who urged them to come to the other side of the island where, they said, their chief lay dying and wished to be baptized. ◦‿Biard and his followers accompanied the Indians down the bay to a spot where the Indian chief lay, legend has it, suffering merely from a head cold, but eager to have the new arrivals settle near his

ISLAND

camp. Champlain had impressed the Indians, and settlers from France were considered desirable neighbors. ∽ Father Biard agreed to the proposal, and Saint-Sauveur was moved to a spot near the present site of Southwest Harbor where the priest and his followers started to build a settlement. Neither the Biard party nor the Indians knew that Captain Samuel Argall of the Virginia Colony had been sent to patrol the coast of New France, which King James I had claimed for England. A month after the arrival of the French, however, Captain Argall heard of the settlers from neighboring Indians, and suspecting who they might be, ran up his battle flags, loaded his cannon, and bore down on Mount Desert Island where the French ship, Jonas, lay anchored off shore. ∽ The engagement was a disaster for the French, and after a brief struggle they surrendered. A young lay priest, Gilbert du Thet, who on leaving home had expressed the desire to die in the service of the church in the New World, got his wish—he was mortally wounded trying to return fire on the British. The fledgling settlement was eventually razed and most of the French taken prisoner and in time allowed to return to their homeland. The skirmish was the first in the 150-year struggle between England and France for control of the North American continent, a contest which culminated in the French and Indian War, and ended with the fall of Quebec in 1759. ∽ Throughout this period Frenchman's Bay served as a staging area for French men-of-war preparing to attack the English. Protected from the Atlantic gales and dotted with mountainous islands behind which even the tallest frigate could hide while being outfitted or repaired, the bay was ideal for the purpose. To it came ships and soldiers from France, among them the dashing

Pierre le Moyne d'Iberville, discoverer of the mouth of the Mississippi, who would wait in the bay to pounce on English ships passing by at sea, and the self-styled nobleman, Antoine de la Mothe Cadillac, believed to have been the model for the central figure in Edmond Rostand's play, Cyrano de Bergerac. Cadillac, in reality an adventurer of humble birth, later founded the settlement that became the city of Detroit and today his self-bestowed coat of arms adorns Cadillac cars. Even after Quebec fell to the British, ringing down the final curtain on French territorial ambitions in North America, French influence played a part in the settlements springing up around the bay. In 1786, at which time a few pioneers of English descent were already established on Mount Desert, Mme. Barthelmy de Gregoire, a granddaughter of Antoine de la Mothe Cadillac, arrived in America claiming title to the island and other land along the bay. The holdings she sought had been granted to her grandfather by the French governor of Canada a hundred years earlier. Mme. de Gregoire carried letters of introduction from Lafayette, and in the climate of friendship with France that existed at the end of the American Revolution, she obtained a favorable hearing and was given citizenship and title to the eastern half of Mount Desert Island. Mme. de Gregoire and her family had no preparation for the rigors of frontier life, but settled nevertheless at Hull's Cove, where they built a crude house and a mill, existing for a few years chiefly on money obtained from selling deeds to land around the bay. Mme. de Gregoire died in 1811; her grave can still be seen, marked by a boulder, in the old burial ground at Hull's Cove. In an era now regarded as having given little consideration to the capabilities of women, it is interesting that

VISION

three Frenchwomen, starting with the Marquise de Guercheville in the 17th century, played notable roles in the history of the bay. A few years after the arrival of Mme. de Gregoire, Mme. Bacler de Leval, a woman of vision and intellectual energy, quit her homeland and came to Mount Desert with a group of friends, planning to establish a center of French civilization in America. She bought land at the head of the bay from her fellow countrywoman, Mme. de Gregoire, and went to work to build a settlement and cultural center there. ◦Traces of Mme. de Leval's dream exist today. Although her settlement was short lived, a number of her followers remained in the area and founded families who rose to prominence in America. One of these, the LaFarge family, included John, the muralist and creator of some of the country's most celebrated stained glass windows, Christopher, a noted architect, and Oliver, an anthropologist and writer. The village of Lamoine is named for a member of Mme. de Leval's group and in it today stands a row of Lombardy poplars grown from cuttings which, according to legend, Madame herself brought from France. In this century another French expatriate, the late Pierre Monteux, conductor of the Boston Symphony Orchestra, founded a summer school of music on land which once belonged to Mme. de Leval. ◦In the century and a half between the destruction of Saint-Sauveur and the fall of Quebec, the cliffs and forests that ring Frenchman's Bay lay in their primeval state, disturbed only by the summer encampments of Abnaki and the occasional forays of ships' crews coming ashore for fresh water from hillside springs or tall trees to replace masts shattered by cannon fire. ◦But after 1760, colonists who were feeling cramped in southern New England

started to look north to lands no longer threatened by French and Indian raids. Of these, a few who had the nerve and brawn to challenge a remote and rugged coast, began to settle on the shores and islands of the bay. Perhaps some had read the list made by an officer on a Massachusetts revenue cutter that visited the bay in 1762, which, in addition to "an extraordinary fine harbor," mentioned: *... oak, beech, maple and all sorts of spruce and pine. Also ash, poplar, birch, white cedar, sassafras, and many other sorts of wood.... Fruits such as raspberrys, strawberrys, cranberrys, gooseberrys and currants ... Its inhabitants of the brute creation: moose, deer, bear, fox, otter, beaver, martins, wild cat, and many other animals of the fur kind, as well as all kinds of wild fowl, hares and partridges ... Codfish in quantitys with very convenient beaches for curing and drying them.... Shellfish of all sorts, fine prawns and shrimp, and a great quantity of pease, sufficient to feed innumerable numbers of herds of cattle ...* To a Massachusetts farmer with 20 or 30 acres of stony pasture and a dozen mouths to feed—and there were many such—the ship's officer's list must have made Frenchman's Bay sound like the promised land. The visit on which it was compiled, however, took place in balmy summer weather. Any settler who came to the bay expecting nature's cornucopia to spill an easy living into his lap soon learned otherwise. Land and sea around the bay yielded their timber and furs and fish only to canny, patient men, willing to endure harsh winters, treacherous seas, and loneliness. But settlers came and, in spite of the rigors, many stayed. Their farms took root according to a pattern: fields were cleared; in two, three, or four years log cabins were replaced with frame houses;

BARNS

then barns were built for animals that had been kept in sheds, and crude, small boats were supplanted by more sophisticated fishing schooners. ◈By the time of the Revolution, settlement around the bay had developed to a point where the farms and ships of local families were attractive targets for English raiders. In a foray in 1781, marines from the British sloop Allegiance burned the home of Captain Daniel Sullivan on Waukeag Neck, now Sorrento, and took the captain prisoner. According to a British Admiralty account taken from the log of the Allegiance, Captain Sullivan tried to bribe the officer to whose charge he was committed with an offer of "his daughter at command," which, according to the log, the virtuous officer "nobly refused, preferring his own station to any rebel General's arms." ◈Whether or not the account of the proffered bribe was true, Sullivan later turned down an offer of parole in exchange for a declaration of allegiance to England. He was imprisoned for 14 months and, when finally released, died on his way home. The town of Sullivan was later named for him and a monument to him stands today in the old burying ground on Waukeag Point. ◈The last decades of the 18th and most of the 19th century were the era of the salt water farm, when settlers who raised their families around Frenchman's Bay made their living from a combination of fishing and farming, with some hunting, trapping, timber cutting, and boat building thrown in. For a number of years after most of the commercially profitable timber had been cut, quarrying, too, was a part time local industry. The salt water farm in time came to symbolize a breed of man—the Downeast Yankee—and a way of life that was part of the American legend, along with the cowpokes and cattle rustlers of the old west

and the plantation hierarchy of the ante-bellum south. ～Today in East Sullivan, Margaret Nickerson Caldwell, a 90-year-old descendant of early settlers, still remembers the time when a man and his sons would set up a cradle by their barn in spring, build a fishing boat, and launch it on a high tide in June from the shore below their house. All life, she recalls, was geared to a seasonal calendar. Spring and summer determined whether a family would live adequately for the rest of the year; if they planted late, or lost a boat, or were hindered by abnormal weather, they might experience real hunger in the cold months. ～Mrs. Caldwell's family caught fish and salted it or smoked it for the winter. They planted peas and corn, pumpkin and squash, turnips, potatoes, beets, cucumbers, and winter beans. They kept a Jersey cow, hens, and sometimes a pig. Their store bills often were no more than four dollars a month. ～In autumn the whole family worked threshing grain with flails and the women shelled beans for winter use. After the first snow had fallen, the men cut the winter's supply of firewood and then headed for back country where tall trees grew, for ship timbers which were dragged back to their farm on ox-drawn sledges. Occasional hunting helped keep the larder stocked; stewed venison was a standard dish which made it possible for the household to feed a shipbuilding crew. ～Groceries for the winter were ordered from the Boston suppliers, E. E. Gray. To eke out what they had grown themselves, the family needed a half barrel each of sugar and oats. No one who could help it risked running out of essential supplies; the possibility of being snowbound was too great. ～Even with enough food and firewood, winters around the bay were long and cold. Houses were banked at their

ROCK

foundations with sod and spruce boughs to block, wherever possible, the sharp, insistent wind that blew down out of the northeast, driving before it great clouds of snow and insinuating white, crystalline ribbons through cracks around windows and under unprotected door jambs. There were times when the ice in Frenchman's Bay reached such thickness that loads of hay could be driven across it by horse and wagon from Sullivan to Bar Harbor. Later, when steamships came into use, old residents remember the steamer Sebenoa ramming through the frozen bay with a man walking ahead, pointing out the dark spots which meant thin ice. ✏ Isolation from medical care made every mother a surrogate doctor. Tansy, pennyroyal, yellowroot, mustard seed for poultices, and a supply of bear's grease and hen's grease were kept on hand for treating common complaints. Actual doctors, if available at all, often could not be reached in time to save the life of someone stricken suddenly. ✏ Today, old-timers who grew up in Hancock at the head of Frenchman's Bay recall Dr. Fred Bridgham being summoned from Sullivan for cases of serious illness. To reach him, a relative or neighbor of the sick person had to travel, probably in a horse-drawn gig, over seven or more miles of rough road and cross a stretch of water on a scow which carried the gig, the driver, and an often reluctant horse. In even earlier times, Dr. Kendall Kittredge, the first physician to serve Mount Desert Island, was sometimes summoned by signal fires. Under these conditions, only children with ample natural good health lived to grow up; the rows of tiny, weathered headstones in each family plot in rural burial grounds around the bay are mute evidence of the great number who died at a young age. ✏ Vessels of all descriptions were built

in local boatyards throughout much of the 19th century. The most famous of the Frenchman's Bay sailing ships was the brig Pilgrim, built on Stave Island, which served as the setting for Richard Henry Dana's classic, *Two Years Before the Mast*. The town of Sullivan alone had four major boatyards and several smaller ones. A visitor in 1837 counted as many as 600 sets of sails on the bay at one time. ~With the coming of steam, the building of larger sailing vessels began to decline. The early steamers that plied the bay must have provoked derisive laughter from skilled hands on the older sailing vessels. The new craft were clumsy and comical looking. One of the earliest, the Buttercup, burned wood for fuel. For the Buttercup to go backward its captain had to stop the engine and start it going the other way. The steamers were an asset, however, to the farmers of Hancock, Sullivan, and Sorrento, enabling them to transport produce quickly and cheaply to markets in Bar Harbor. ~In the past hundred years, the hamlets of Frenchman's Bay have reversed the pattern of most early towns and villages. Instead of growing, commerce and industry around the once lively harbor have declined. Wharves and ways that were crowded with workmen, sailors, and supplies in the days of sailing vessels have disappeared and the shore they occupied has been reclaimed by the forest. Today there are many spots around the bay from which only the majestic wilderness described by Champlain in 1604 can be seen. It is hard for a present-day visitor to imagine the earlier scene, with shipbuilding going on in every cove and loads of barrel staves, granite, and fish leaving the bay for markets in Portland, Boston, and New York on each high tide. ~About the time that shipbuilding began to decline and the craftsmen who built

TIME

the old wooden sailing vessels were turning to other means of livelihood, a new wave of settlers started to appear around the bay. These were well-to-do families from Boston, New York, and Philadelphia, who came to see the mountains and bay, and stayed to buy land and build summer houses. Ironically, these folk, many of whom were seeking an escape from the hectic life of established watering places, ended by making Bar Harbor and its environs into a resort area that ranked with the already famous Newport, Rhode Island, and Saratoga, New York. ∽ The first summer visitors were artists of the Hudson River school, Thomas Cole, William Hart, and Frederick E. Church among them, who explored the Maine coast in search of new subjects and were captivated by Frenchman's Bay. Their descriptions of the scenery and paintings brought others to the bay in their footsteps. ∽ After the artists came doctors, educators, lawyers, and financiers. Most of the summer residents were also sportsmen, and shared an interest in the sea. It was an era when there was great enthusiasm for hiking, mountain climbing, rowing, and sailing. For several years, starting in 1871, Colonel Albert Stickney of Boston and Dr. Robert Derby of New York rowed a skiff from Boston to Bar Harbor to join their summering families and friends. Their annual arrival at the pier in Bar Harbor attracted crowds from around the bay and was looked forward to as an event of the summer season. ∽ Early residents of the summer colony included college presidents Charles W. Eliot of Harvard and Seth Low of Columbia; the Episcopal Bishop of Albany, William Croswell Doane; and Joseph H. Curtis, an eminent landscape architect. Many in this first wave of summer residents spent a season or two at one of several boarding houses and hotels that sprang

up around the bay. Guests in these establishments were classified as "mealers" or "hauled mealers" by the proprietors depending on whether they were staying or merely coming to dine. The bay's reputation for fine sailing and an invigorating climate spread rapidly, and the summer colony swelled to include Vanderbilts, Morgans, Biddles, Rockefellers, Fords, and other families connected with financial and industrial power. These magnates built houses on islands in the bay or along "millionaires' row" between Bar Harbor and Salisbury Cove, boosting the local economy with their lavish entertaining. A number of clubs whose names were to become bywords were founded as the resort grew—among them the Kebo Valley Golf Club and the Bar Harbor Reading Room, a men's sanctuary where much of the reading in the prohibition era was said to have been done through the bottom of a glass. In Salisbury Cove, the visitors' book at the Pot and Kettle Club bears the signatures of five presidents. William Howard Taft, Warren Harding, Theodore and Franklin Roosevelt and Harry Truman were all guests there on at least one occasion, as was John Kennedy during his time in the Senate. The concentration of financial power in the hands of Pot and Kettle Club members was so great, observers said, that presidents were at least as gratified to be entertained there as the financiers and industrialists were to receive them. For many years Joseph Pulitzer, owner of the New York World, spent summers at Chatwold, the mansion he built on Mount Desert Island. The publisher had become acutely sensitive to noise and spent much of his time at Chatwold in an elaborately constructed "tower of silence" whose walls were impenetrable to sound. John D. Rockefeller Jr. summered a few miles away in a 107-room house

BIRDS

called Eyrie. Evelyn Walsh McLean, owner of the ill-omened 44-carat Hope Diamond had a house on Bar Harbor's Shore Path, and nearby, Mrs. Edward Stotesbury gave parties on a scale that required the ordering of champagne glasses through a local emporium in lots of 50 dozen. ⤴This opulence was a contrast to the spare, thrifty way of life that dominated Frenchman's Bay before summer people came. Among some of the bay's Yankee families, the tradition of fishing and farming for a living gave way to tending flower beds and carrying tea trays. Others took jobs manning the many yachts based in the bay, or opened stores catering to the summer colony's wants. Many, however, continued in their old occupations of fishing, carpentry, and other crafts, and largely ignored the changes that accompanied the new arrivals. ⤴One lasting benefit came about as a result of the summer settlement: the creation of Acadia National Park. Groundwork for the park was laid in 1901 when George Buckman Dorr of Boston and Dr. Charles W. Eliot, then president emeritus of Harvard, started a drive to protect the land around the bay from commercial exploitation. Both men were long-time summer residents of Mount Desert Island, devoted to its scenery and fond of tramping its trails. Their efforts succeeded in bringing some 6000 acres on the island into a public trust. ⤴Later, in 1919, Acadia became the first national park east of the Rockies. Now, extended by land gifts from John D. Rockefeller Jr. and others, it covers 41,645 acres and includes part of the Schoodic Peninsula and Isle au Haut to the south. The park shelters the only remaining stand of first growth spruce on the Maine coast and over 500 other species of plant life, as well as some 300 different birds, including barred and great horned owls, peregrine falcons,

migrating arctic terns, golden plovers, and other increasingly rare species. ⌒ The park lies at what is, botanically, a crossroads of the temperate, the Canadian, and the Arctic zones. Arctic plants spread south millions of years ago in the frigid belt that preceded the glacier, and remained, after the ice sheet melted, in spots too exposed to support other growth. Most of these plants are tough, wiry creepers. They include the black crowberry, the baked-apple berry, creeping juniper, mountain cranberry, Alpine bearberry, and roseroot. Many of them can be seen in the Wild Gardens of Acadia, a small, cultivated area in the park where specimens of indigenous plants grow in conditions matching their natural habitat. ⌒ Because of the tempering effect of the ocean, the park is also the northernmost point at which some southern plants are found. A grove of scrub oak on the side of Acadia Mountain belongs to a species found nowhere else on the Atlantic coast north of Long Island. Pitch pine, sweet pepperbush, viburnum, and swamp loosestrife are also native to the park. ⌒ The park's Robert Abbe Museum houses a collection of artifacts from successive Indian cultures that have existed around Frenchman's Bay. Stone Age Indians known as the Red Paint People left sharp, delicate stone tools which have been unearthed in various locations. Pottery and copper tools from a later culture have been found in the deep shell heaps accumulated by early people along the shore. The Abnaki, the most recent Indians to inhabit the region, also left shell heaps in spots where they came for feasts which must have been the forerunners of present-day clambakes. The Abnaki made watertight baskets in which they could boil food, and were wood craftsmen, producing birch bark canoes strong enough to travel

TRACES

far out to sea. ⟿ In 1947, portions of the park were severely damaged in what was probably the most extensively reported and photographed forest fire the country has ever seen. The fire started in late October at a dump on the outskirts of Bar Harbor. Swept along at times by gale force winds, travelling underground through dry, rocky terrain at other times, the fire raged for days, crisscrossing Mount Desert Island as the wind shifted. Men who fought the flames compared them to a giant blow torch, constantly fanned by the wind. Fleeing the inferno, rabbits and other small animals were seen seeking shelter in ditches or near streams in the company of predators like wildcats and foxes. ⟿ The fire pre-empted newspaper space on front pages all over the western world, so great was the fame of the Bar Harbor summer resort. Bar Harbor itself and some surrounding hamlets were evacuated before the fire finally burned itself out in a tremendous column of flame that reached a mile out over the water of Frenchman's Bay at Great Head. ⟿ Comparatively few of the park's wild animals perished in the fire. The great casualties were trees—timber was destroyed over almost a third of Mount Desert Island, the Bar Harbor summer colony —where five hotels and many homes were leveled, and the Jackson Laboratory, where important cancer research was going on at the time. Only chimneys and garden statuary were left standing on several of the resort's great estates. Fashionable life had been gradually curtailed by increased taxes in the years preceding the fire, and the holocaust contributed to its further decline. ⟿ Much has changed around the bay in recent years, but the most significant landmarks are little altered. Bar Harbor is still an active summer community although its orientation is different from

pre-World War II days. Many of the great houses that survived the fire have been converted to schools and other public uses, and a concentration of new motels cluster around the approaches to Mount Desert Island and Bar Harbor itself. Jackson Laboratories has risen from the ashes with superbly equipped new buildings and now specializes in the field of mammalian genetics. The boats that stand at anchor off the Bar Harbor shore today are smaller than J. P. Morgan's Corsair and the other magnates' yachts that dominated the bay in the early years of the century, but many pleasure craft still head for Mount Desert in the summer. In Acadia National Park, dirt and gravel roads have been paved and a few refinements of an informational nature, such as auto tape tours, added, but the mountains and ponds and plant life are unchanged. The scars of the fire have healed more rapidly than naturalists predicted, and timber growth is gradually replacing the trees that were leveled in 1947. In the smaller communities around the bay, the commerce and industry of the 19th century are all but extinct, with forest growth and winter storms having obliterated traces of the docks and boatyards that once lined the shore. But fishermen still tie up at a number of little wooden piers at Sorrento, Winter Harbor and other hamlets, and through the trees around the shore, the functional houses of a new generation of summer residents can occasionally be glimpsed. On farms around the bay, tractors now do the work of oxen. Self-sustaining homesteads are a thing of the past, and a farm family's grocery bills today amount to considerably more than the four or five-dollar-a-month expenditure of the salt water farm era. There are still places, however, where the danger of being cut off from the nearest community

FOCUS

exists in winter blizzards. And, in exposed locations, houses continue to be banked with fir boughs in November for protection against the wind and snow. ∽Several granges are active around the bay. Farmers gather twice a month to share agricultural information and take part in a simple, symbolic ritual. The granges are modest buildings, but are well cared for, and serve as a social center for their members. ∽Lobsters, commercially the bay's most valuable seafood, are the focus of a fishing industry which, like farming, occupies fewer people than it used to. Lobsters were once so abundant that settlers picked them up from the beaches to use as fertilizer, but their numbers have declined because, in the past, too many were taken. Shrimp, a tiny Maine variety, are now a second important market catch. ∽The faces of the fishermen who head out to sea in the early morning darkness to pull their lobster traps are often remarkably like those of forbears pictured in daguerrotypes on the parlor walls of their homes. Around the bay there is a phrase "tough it out alone," meaning to bear one's troubles oneself, which is what these men do. ∽As for the bay itself, "the more things change other places, the more the bay stays the same," a long-absent native is supposed to have said on his return. Perhaps he was right. Changes on the bay seem to be those which hardly count as change at all: the shift of clouds, the slow dispersal of fog under a summer sun, the sudden plunge of a herring gull after fish, the breaking of surf on the outer headlands, and the sudden cry of a loon.

The bay from Cadillac Mountain: behind these islands in the 17th and 18th centuries French warriors like Pierre le Moyne d'Iberville waited with men-of-war to pounce on English ships passing by at sea.

"The sea endlessly destroys and rebuilds the land," the Acadia National Park Service tells visitors. "It lifts giant granite blocks and tumbles them onto the shore; it carves caves and chasms in the rock; and while the sea destroys, it also deposits new beaches on the altered shore." Here, the surf-scoured rock of Schoodic Point is evidence of the ocean's power.

OVERLEAF: *Ironbound Island.*

"Red sky at night, sailors' delight" an old folk saying asserts. Lambent clouds reflecting a sunset on the bay promise fair weather for the next day.

An offshore ledge and jagged cliff on Ironbound Island present an inhospitable face to the passing sailor.

Fish weirs are still maintained in a few places around the bay although they are less common than they used to be. This weir is in Winter Harbor, a deep, sheltered cove which has never frozen over.

July meadows are bright with black-eyed Susans and other wildflowers.

*Looking toward Schoodic Mountain
from Cadillac Mountain: a part of the bay
that is little changed today from
the wilderness Champlain described in 1604.*

Self-assured but watchful, a gull keeps one eye on the camera.

The moon streaks a bright path across Sorrento Harbor.

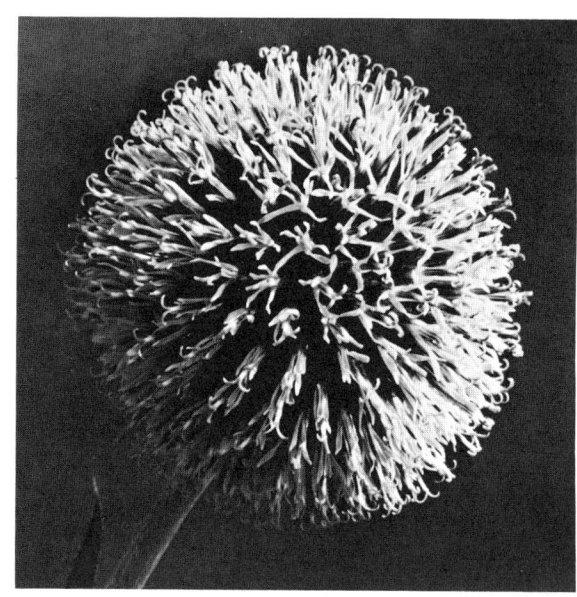

Globe thistles bloom around the bay in August and September.

Weather is mercurial on the bay.
Fog banks materialize suddenly, seeming to come from nowhere.

Shell and barnacle clusters form patterns on mud at low tide.

Hog Bay marshes: bulrushes stand erect but softer grasses bend in a summer breeze.

LEFT: *July wildflowers bloom in a meadow beside the bay.*

Once prized by Indian basket makers who used to visit the bay, bulrushes now serve decorative purposes in dried grass arrangements for winter bouquets.

OVERLEAF: *Scoured by surf-born sand and pebbles, the granite shores of Grindstone Neck have been worn smooth over millions of years.*

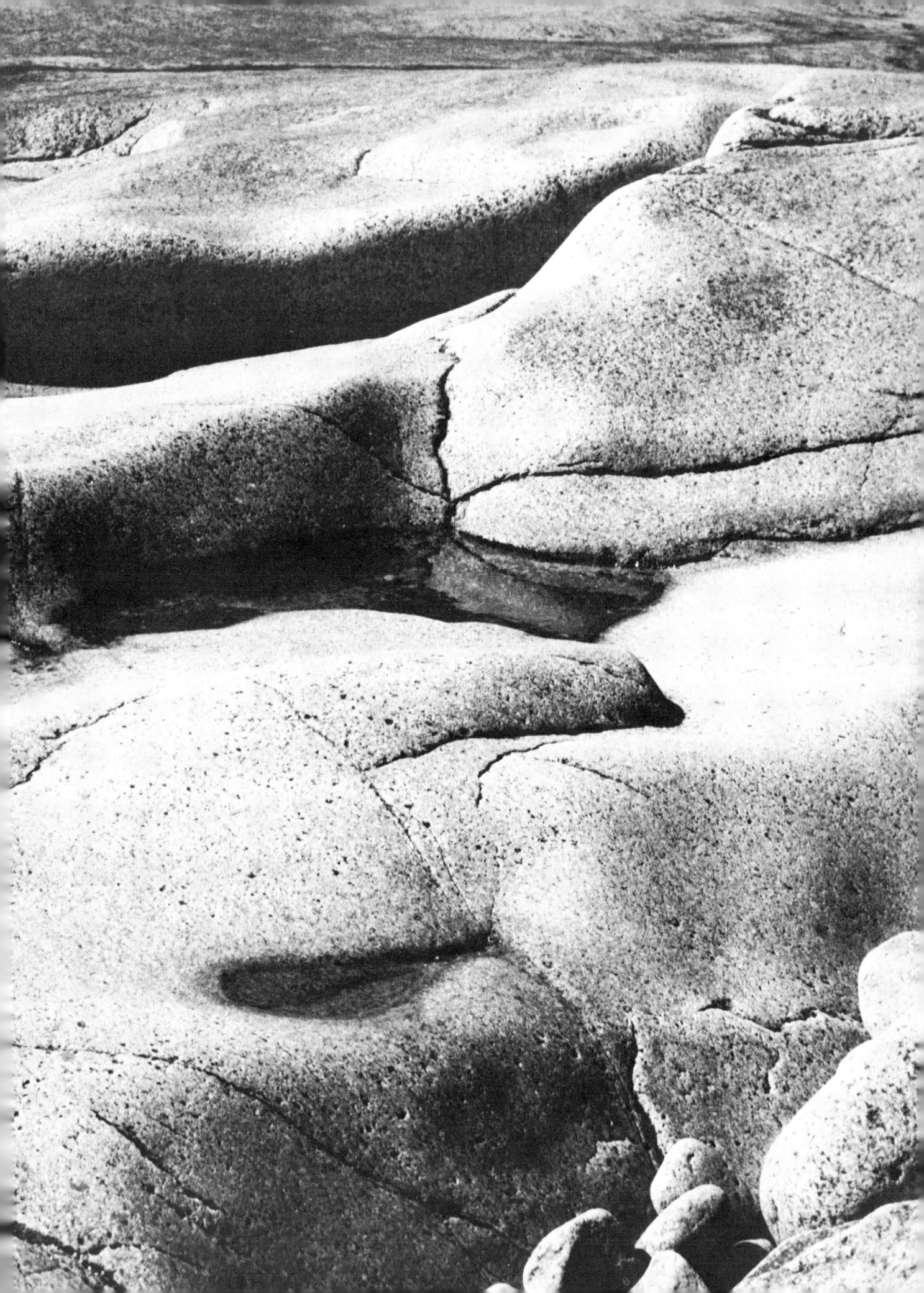

Bladder wrack, a form of seaweed.

A Friendship sloop being stored for the winter. These strong, handsome sailboats built in the seacoast town of Friendship, near Rockland, were originally designed for fishing and lobstering but are now in demand as pleasure craft.

Cormorants perch on a rock in the bay.

LEFT: *If you drive north along the Maine coast toward Frenchman's Bay, you will see the white sand beaches and seaward-sloping meadows gradually disappear and the upland woods of oak and maple give way to a dark northern forest of spruce and fir, reaching to the water's edge. Along the bay's shore, the contrast of brooding forest and bright water is sharpened by granite headlands where light and shadow accent the rocks' geometry.*

The Mount Desert range, seen from Sullivan at the head of the bay.

Schoodic Point: a determined tree sustains itself on the soil and water collected in a narrow crevice in the rock.

Seaside roses display shiny hips when summer bloom is over.

Fingers of rock extend into the bay from the Schoodic Peninsula.

Morning fog dissipates at Sorrento Harbor.

Forms of life adapted to both air and water live in the intertidal zone. These plants and animals are tough and resilient: they withstand pounding surf and exposure to the scorching summer sun. Here, barnacles and rockweed mingle to form a pattern at low tide.

OVERLEAF: *Discarded lobster pot buoys bleach in the sun. Buoys used to mark the location of lobster pots are painted, like ancient heraldry, in each fisherman's individual colors.*

Calf Island landscape: a study in textures.

LEFT: *It takes more than rocks and shade to stifle growth. This tree's roots twisted and spread until they reached soil and water.*

Weathered board sheds are common in every hamlet around the bay. Simple, low-hung buildings, they often blend into a background of dark spruce and fir as unobtrusively as does this boatyard on the waterfront.

International Mercury class race at Frenchman's Bay, 1972.

A lonely farmhouse at Lamoine.

This imposing turn-of-the-century house in Sorrento was built by a summer resident next door to his own house. It was for his wife, whose company he apparently found uncongenial. Old-timers who remember the couple recall the mansion's mistress driving "hell worse'n crooked" through the little town's streets in her horse and gig.

Bell tower of the Episcopal church in Sorrento.

The influx of summer residents that started in the 1880s eventually led to the building of several new churches in hamlets around the bay. Like most churches dating from the turn of the century, they were quite different from the simple white clapboard buildings of earlier Maine tradition. This steeple, which seems to combine features from a number of different architectural periods, belongs to the Episcopal church in Sorrento.

"High Seas," a tapestry brick mansion overlooking the bay just outside Bar Harbor, was built in 1912 by a German emigre for his future wife who was coming from Europe to marry him. The bride-to-be drowned on the Titanic and the house passed to a succession of owners. It now belongs to Jackson Laboratories, a Bar Harbor research institute, and is used to house students who work in the institute's summer program.

OVERLEAF: *A Winter Harbor lobster boat stands on the shingle at low tide.*

Lobster traps piled on the shore at Winter Harbor. Traps used today are built according to a design that dates back to the 1670s.

Lobsters fresh from the sea and full of fight travel to a pound in the bottom of a local lobsterman's boat. Their snapping claws are fastened to prevent the strong ones from attacking weaker specimens; one lobster can cut another in half. Elastic bands are now used to close the claws instead of the older wooden pegs which sometimes damaged edible portions. Lobstering still provides a living for some families around Frenchman's Bay although the catch has declined in recent years.

LEFT: *East Franklin, overlooking an arm of Hog Bay.*

Dancing on a homemade rig, two sturdy mackerel are pulled in by a bay fisherman.

Summertime: children fishing off a dock on the Taunton River.

Egg Rock Light, established in 1875, marks the entrance to Frenchman's Bay.

OVERLEAF: *A Sorrento lobsterman, his bait barrel behind him, tidies his boat after the day's haul has been unloaded. His work started in the dark hours of early morning when he headed out to his traps several miles away. Each lobsterman's traps are grouped in "stringers" attached to a single line which is marked at each end by buoys painted in his colors. The traps are hauled aboard with a winch powered by the boat's engine, and the legal lobsters removed. Females with eggs must be returned to the ocean, as must oversize lobsters and immature ones. Traps are rebaited with fish as each is emptied; then the boat is started up and the traps go back into the ocean, either in the same location if it was successful, or in a new one.*

Over the years, builders around the bay have relied on their own imagination and the materials at hand to express their individuality. This dormered, gabled house in Winter Harbor wears a variety of applied decorations including inset panels of cement studded with pebbles under the eaves.

A gable on a Sorrento house has its own small balcony.

This summer resident of Grindstone Neck liked lighthouses and built his own house to look like one.

LEFT: *Entrance gate to "The Turrets," an empty Bar Harbor mansion.*

"The Turrets" is a relic of turn of the century grandeur, as the date over its porte-cochere indicates. It was designed by Bruce Price, the architect for Quebec's Chateau Frontenac, and is characteristic of the summer homes that lined Bar Harbor's Ocean Drive and Shore Path up to the time of World War II. Built in the style of European villas and manor houses, they contained grand staircases, elaborate panelling, many massive fireplaces, conservatories, butlers' pantries with shelf space for a dozen dinner services, wine cellars, safes, and often servants quarters as cramped and gloomy as the main house was splendid. Many of the surviving Bar Harbor mansions have been given over to public uses and now house inns, exhibits, or schools like the Ecole Acadie and the College of the Atlantic.

Calf Island, looking toward Little Calf, crowned with dark spruce, and tiny Thrumcap. The land to the left of Thrumcap is Stave Island, named in the period when barrel staves were the basis for an important industry. The brig Pilgrim, the setting for Richard Henry Dana's sea classic TWO YEARS BEFORE THE MAST, *was built on Stave Island.*

Calf Island: tall spruce and a tiny cottage cast long reflections across the bay on a tranquil day.

Reflections of the past glimmer in the window of an empty store in Winter Harbor.

LEFT: *Summer settlement around the bay began in an era when family worship was an important part of daily life. Private chapels were not as uncommon then as they are today. This rustic building sheltered in deep woods on Calf Island was a chapel built by the family who owned the island and summered there many years ago.*

A stained glass window in the door of the private chapel on Calf Island.

OVERLEAF: *A Lobster boat tied up near Long Cove.*

Dories loaded with herring nets and lobster boats in Winter Harbor.

LEFT: *Ferns edge the woods like lacy collars.*

The Episcopal church in Winter Harbor.

A sturdy church in Winter Harbor.

Winter Harbor: in spite of the shallows in the foreground, the mean depth of this harbor is 42 feet.

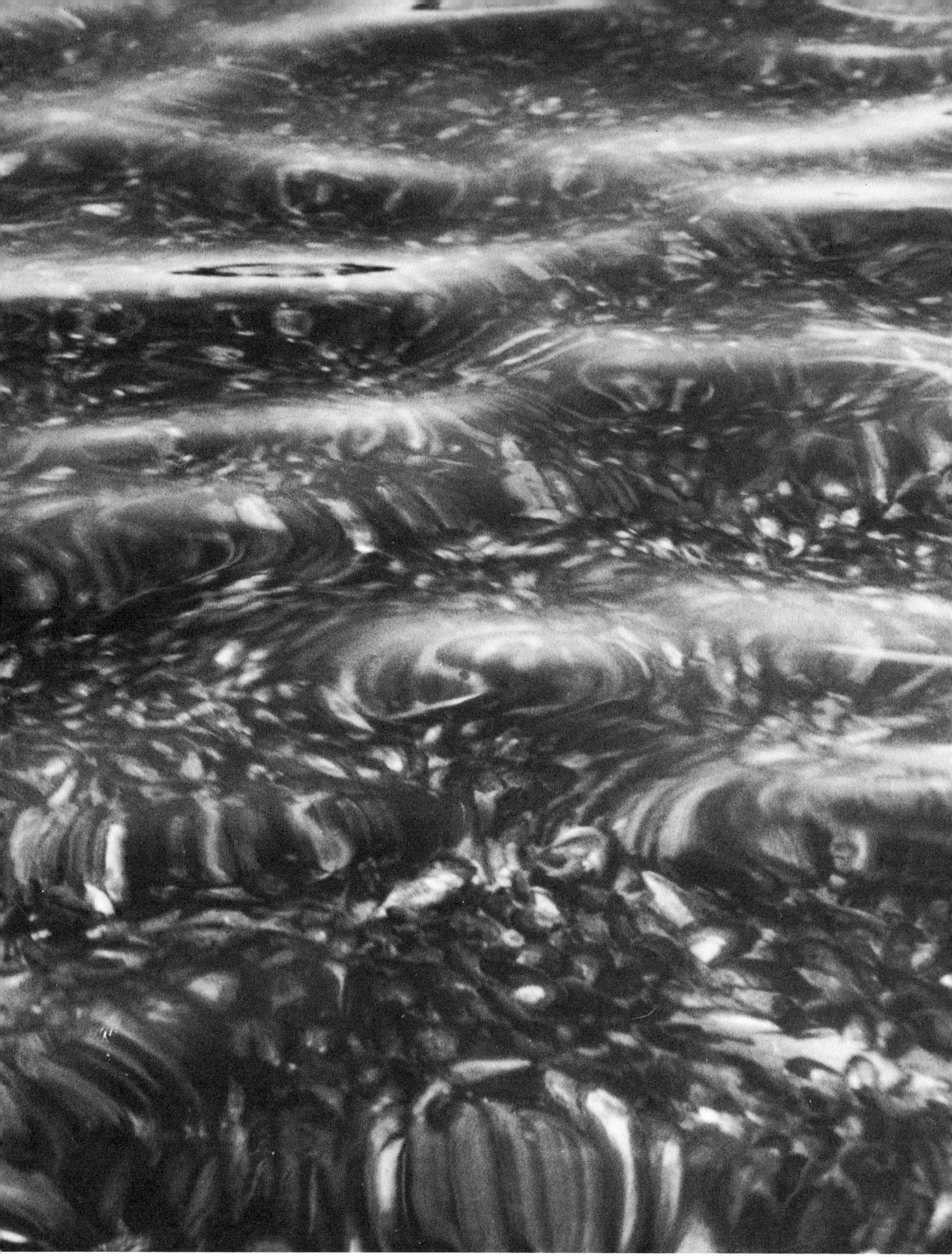

Mussel beds, marbled by the undulating current of Flanders Bay.

Lobster boats, in from the day's work, moored in harbor.

LEFT: *Sloops moored after a cruise up the coast.*

This memorandum of agreement for building a vessel, entered into this 13th day of January 1866 between Messrs West & Card of Franklin. Me., party of the first, and Joseph Wass of Milbridge Me. and the other parties signing this document in connection with him of the second part witnesseth.

That we, J. H. West and Wm H. Card of Franklin Me. agree to build and complete a vessel, including spars, said vessel to be hermaphrodite-brig rigged, (double top-sail yards,) of not less than two hundred, or more than two hundred and twenty tons, old custom house measurement, and of the following dimensions and materials. Tonnage to be ascertained, as the Government Surveyor of the District of Frenchman's Bay usually measures vessels; said vessel to be single-deck, and of the following dimensions. Length over all one hundred feet; breadth of beam twenty-eight feet; depth of hold, nine feet or thereabout. To iron all the spars, strap all blocks, and also the iron work on the hull, such as lower dead eyes, chain plates, ring bolts, eyebolts, heart and bulls eyes that are attached to the head gear; to furnish patent windlass, wheel, bobstay, pumps and davits. The top timbers to be hackmatack, upper foothook of old growth pine, the balance of the frame of beach, birch and maple; top thick-streak, to be of hard wood, six inches thick, and from eight to ten inches wide; beams and clamps to be of Norway pine, also the ceiling, down to the thick streak; the balance of the ceiling to be of hard wood; hackmatack knees of suitable dimensions to be used throughout; said vessel to have hanging knees.

the rest of the spars to be of Spruce.

LEFT: *A page from an 1866 agreement between William Henry Card and a companion shipbuilder, a Mr. West of Franklin, to build a hermaphrodite brig for Joseph Ware of Milbridge and five other owners. Mr. Ware was to be a one-quarter partner in the venture, with the others owning shares of one eighth and one sixteenth each. The ship's cost was to be determined by its final tonnage at the rate of $44 a ton and was required to weigh between 200 and 220 tons when complete. The document is characteristic of shipbuilding arrangements around the bay in the 19th century. It begins:*

This memorandum of agreement for building a vessel, entered into this 12th day of January 1866 between Messrs. West & Card of Franklin, Me., party of the first, and Joseph Ware of Milbridge Me. and the other parties signing this document in connection with him of the second part. Witnesseth, That we, J. H. West and Wm. H. Card of Franklin, Me. agree to build and complete a vessel, including spars, said vessel to be hermophrodite-brig rigged, (double topsail yards) of not less than two-hundred, or more than two hundred and twenty tons, old Customhouse measurement, and of the following dimensions and materials. Tonnage to be ascertained, as the government surveyor of the District of Frenchmans Bay usually measures vessels; said vessel to be singledeck, and of the following dimensions. Length over all, one hundred feet; breadth of beam, twenty-eight feet; depth of hold, nine feet or thereabouts; To iron all the spars, strap all blocks and also the iron work on the hull, such as lower dead eyes, chain plates, ring bolts, eye bolts, hearts and bulls eyes that are attached to the head gear; to furnish patent windlass, wheel bobstays, pumps and davits. The top timbers to be hackmatack, upper foothooks of old growth pine, the balance of the frame of beach, birch and maple; six thick-streaks, to be of hard wood, six inches thick, and from eight to ten inches wide; beams and clamps to be of Norway-pine, also the ceiling, down to the thick-streaks; the balance of the ceiling to be of hard wood; hackmatack knees of suitable dimensions to be used throughout; said vessel to have hanging knees.

Margaret Nickerson Caldwell, descendant of a seafaring family which has lived around the bay for over 200 years, remembers the time when a man and his sons would build a fishing boat by their barn in spring and launch it on a high tide from their own shore in June. A sixth generation descendant of a first settler of nearby Franklin, Mrs. Caldwell grew up able to name all the sails on a clipper ship. Her grandfather, William Henry Card, was a shipbuilder and her father, Thomas Nelson Nickerson, a boss rigger on clippers.

Woodworking is a skill that dates from the early days of settlement around Frenchman's Bay. Prescott Briggs, a Sorrento carpenter and cabinetmaker, carries on the tradition of his forefathers.

LEFT: *A little of everything, including old and not-so-old domestic utensils, is on display at this antique barn in Asheville.*

Using his hands and simple tools, Vibert creates a saucer effect at the base of a bowl . . .

. . . and smoothes the rim of a taller piece.

LEFT: *A number of potters have settled around the bay. Here Dennis Vibert of West Sullivan shapes a vase on his wheel.*

OVERLEAF: *Baseball: if it lands in the bay it's a home run.*

Rocks, just below the surface in Taunton Bay, provide a perch for these harbor seals basking in the sun.

Harbor seals, natural clowns, cavort on Half Tide Ledge.

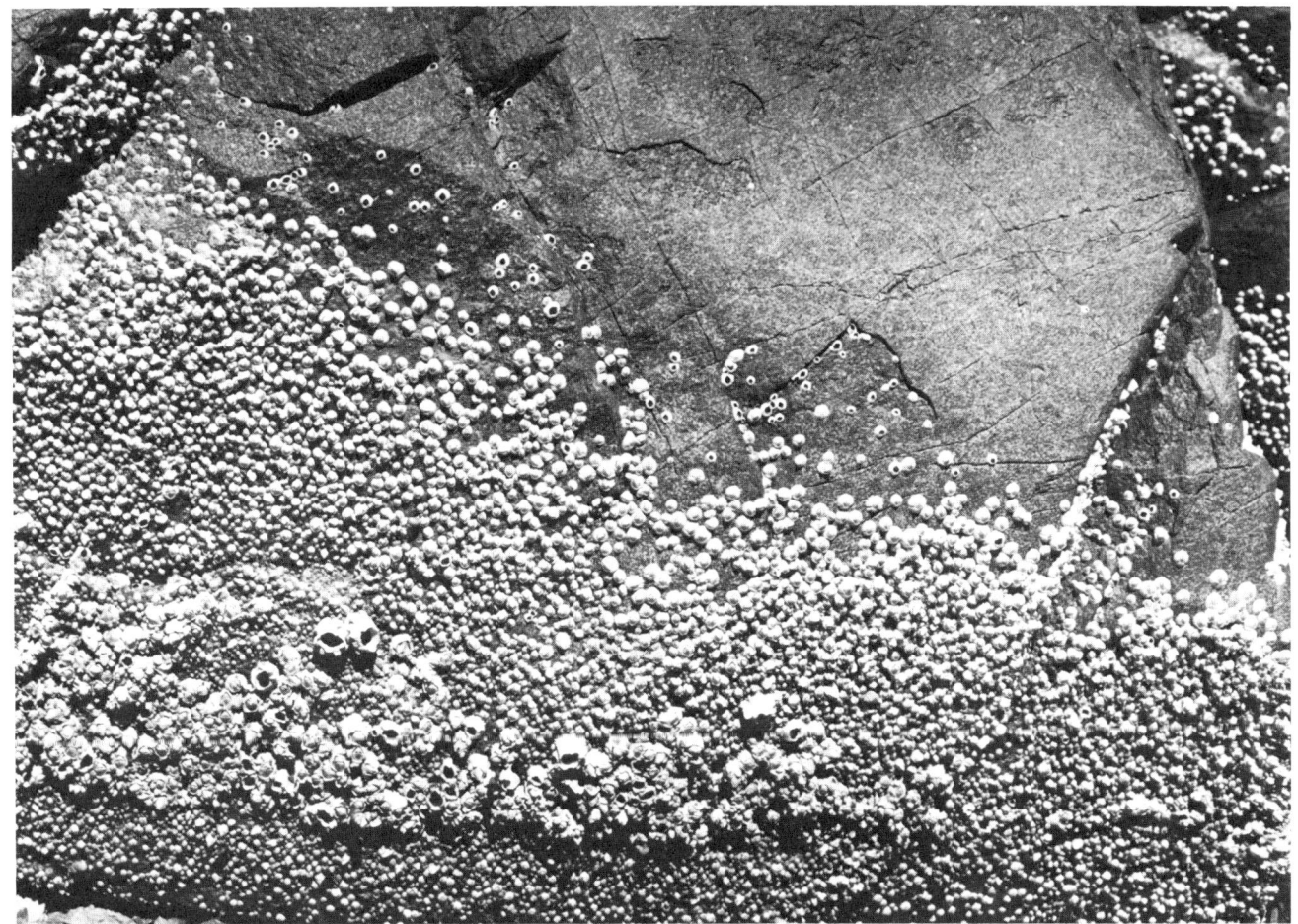

Rock barnacles encrust a boulder at the water's edge.

Like a flagpole sitter, this young osprey perches on the edge of its untidy but commodious nest, looking down the bay for a sign of its mother returning with food.

LEFT: *Between the tides: clamdiggers at Long Cove.*

OVERLEAF: *Thrumcap Island, a bank of sand and rock with little soil, is gradually being washed away in storms.*

This fine old house in Sullivan has an interesting fanlight and front door detail.

This 11-rank player organ now standing in a house in Sorrento is one of a handful built by Aeolian in 1906 as presentation pieces. Recipients included Mark Twain, Pope Pius X, King Edward VII of England, and the Drexel family of Philadelphia.

Around Frenchman's Bay, nothing is far from the forest. The buildings of this farm in Lamoine are sharply silhouetted against a background of spruce and fir.

A double entrance and unusual front windows distinguish this church in Lamoine.

Milking time: a young herdsman takes charge in North Lamoine.

Cat o'nine tails growing through abandoned lobster pots at Sullivan Falls.

A house in Hancock with unusual door detail and leaded lights in the upper portions of its windows.

Sieur de Monts Spring: Indian paths led to this spring on Mt. Desert Island for thousands of years before the first white men came. Now a focal point in Acadia National Park, it has been enclosed and named for the French nobleman under whose auspices Samuel de Champlain explored the bay in 1604.

LEFT: *One sure thing about weather on the bay at any given time is that it will soon change. Here dark clouds pile up suddenly over Partridge Cove.*

The Bar Harbor waterfront.

Sloop cruising past Preble Island.

The Canadian National "Bluenose" Ferry runs between Bar Harbor and Yarmouth, Nova Scotia.

OVERLEAF: *A doe in Acadia National Park pauses in gentle surprise to study the photographer.*

A farmhouse on Schieffelin Point.

LEFT: *An empty house in Winter Harbor,
a relic of bygone summers,
slumbers in the sun.*

Bunchberry in the woods in August.

In September and October, starlike, branching asters bloom in the swamps and meadows.

The bay's answer to the Loch Ness monster? Actually, it's a whale that has been sighted a number of times by boats and from points along the shore.

Hay is baled and carted away for storage on a farm in Trenton.

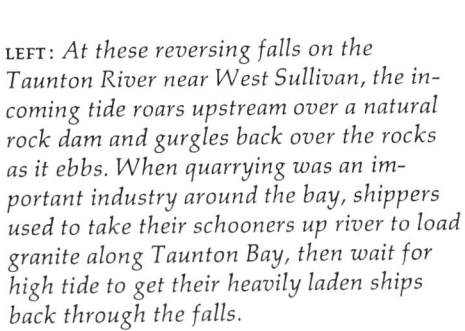

LEFT: At these reversing falls on the Taunton River near West Sullivan, the incoming tide roars upstream over a natural rock dam and gurgles back over the rocks as it ebbs. When quarrying was an important industry around the bay, shippers used to take their schooners up river to load granite along Taunton Bay, then wait for high tide to get their heavily laden ships back through the falls.

A Sorrento-built lobster boat, up for an overhauling in its home port.

"The hills rock-ribb'd and ancient as the sun" in the poem THANATOPSIS *by William Cullen Bryant might be the glacier-formed "Bubbles" beside Jordan Pond in Acadia National Park.*

This harborside summer house in Sorrento was built as a steamship freight office in the days when supplies moved up and down the bay by water instead of circling it by road.

A stone house perched on the rocky shore of Jordan Island.

Seclusion: a house on Spectacle Island in Frenchman's Bay.

From Cadillac Mountain: the entrance to Frenchman's Bay spread out under the ever-changing North Atlantic sky.

THE PHOTOGRAPHER:

Ted Van Winkle, a retired advertising executive, has been photographing most of his life. He has illustrated and written articles for magazines, exhibited his work in the Abercrombie & Fitch Gallery and the Southern Vermont Artists show, and has published a book on the historic town of Bedford, New York, where he lives. He used Kodak Plus-X film and a Pentax camera with a variety of lenses and filters.

THE AUTHOR:

Elizabeth Simonoff is the New England wife of a book publisher and mother of two children, and currently lives in Chappaqua, New York. Originally an editorial researcher for The Reader's Digest, free lance writer and editor for several publishers, she is now a feature writer for the award winning bi-weekly newspaper, The Patent Trader.

THE BOOK:

This book is printed on Mohawk Superfine paper, high finish, 80 pound text.
Text type is 12 on 15 point Palatino Roman.
Design is by Peter Good, production supervision by Raymond Grimaila, and production by Connecticut Printers Incorporated.

This memorandum of
a vessel, entered into
between Mess. West & Co.
of the first, and Joseph
and the other parties se[cond]
connection with him of t[he]

That we, J. H. West a[nd]
Me. agree to build and
spars, said vessel to b[e]
rigged, (double top-sail
two-hundred, or more
twenty tons, old Custom
and of the following
Tonnage to be ascertain[ed]
Surveyor of the District